TEDDY BEARS

Judy Sparrow

SMITHMARK

This edition published in 1993
by SMITHMARK Publishers Inc.
16 East 32nd Street
New York, New York 10016.

SMITHMARK books are available for bulk purchase for sales promotion and premium use. For details write or telephone the Manager of Special Sales, SMITHMARK Publishers Inc., 16 East 32nd Street, New York, NY 10016, (212) 532 6600

Produced by Brompton Books Corp.,
15 Sherwood Place,
Greenwich, CT 06830

ISBN 0-8317-3382-9

Printed in Hong Kong

10 9 8 7 6 5 4 3 2 1

Page 1: This cinammon bear was probably manufactured by the Gaeltarra Eireann company who also traded under the name Tara Toys. He has wood wool throughout his head and body and a small red-and-white foot label reading 'Made in the Republic of Ireland; before 1949 it would have read 'Made in Eire.'

Right: These three bears are typical war-time teddies. The small bear (left; height: 12 inches [31 cm]) is still wearing his original knitted clothes. He was probably made from an old blanket as fur fabrics had become scarce. The bear in the green velvet suit, Newie (center; height: 12 inches [31 cm]), has fur on his head, paws, and feet, although there was not enough available to make his body, which is also of velvet beneath his suit. The gray bear, Plummy (right; height: 14 inches [36 cm]), is another home-made teddy from around 1943. Possibly he was made from an old coat, and has leather pads stitched on top of the fabric, with a very simple jointing mechanism. Although he has some moth holes he has survived very well.

Contents

INTRODUCTION
The Birth of the Teddy Bear

The story of the origins of the teddy bear is now almost legendary, America and Germany both having justifiable claims to be the 'birthplace of the teddy bear.' Although toy bears, often made from real fur, were being made late in the nineteenth century, the jointed teddy is an invention of the twentieth.

America's claim centers around the story of November 1902 when President Theodore 'Teddy' Roosevelt was on a hunting expedition in Mississippi. After an unsuccessful day, one of Roosevelt's aides came across a lost bear cub; he tied the unfortunate creature to a tree so that the President could shoot it and thereby gain another trophy for his hunting lodge. But the President was appalled and ordered the cub to be released. The magnanimity of the gesture achieved instant fame and inspired a popular cartoon by Clifford K Berryman entitled 'Drawing the Line in Mississippi' (below right).

Among the many people to see the cartoon was Morris Michtom, a Russian immigrant running a small candy store in Brooklyn, New York. As a sideline to their main business, he and his wife often made dolls and toys to sell in the shop. When he saw the cartoon, Michtom was inspired to make a jointed toy replica of Roosevelt's bear cub out of brown plush material. He placed the bear in his shop window alongside a copy of the Berryman cartoon and a small notice reading 'Teddy's Bear.'

By the end of the day Michtom had not only sold the bear but also had orders for a dozen more. Within a year Michtom had founded the Ideal Novelty and Toy Company, and the teddy bear was sweeping America. By the time of Michtom's death in 1938, the Ideal Company had become one of the world's leading toy manufacturers.

Despite the fame of the Roosevelt story, and the part it played in the origin of the name, the creation of the first teddy bear is often attributed to Margarete Steiff. Although wheelchair-bound from childhood polio, she founded the Steiff company in 1880 and it soon gained a reputation for making high-quality toy animals. She was assisted in running the company by relatives including her nephew, Richard Steiff. In search of new ideas for the Steiff toy range, he hit upon the idea of a toy bear that could be a boys' equivalent for the ever-popular girls' doll. Richard spent many hours studying bears in Stuttgart Zoo. Late in 1902 he presented his aunt with plans for a bear-like toy with jointed limbs and head. Margarete made up a prototype from scraps of fabric, and the small creature, named Friend Petz, was exhibited on the Steiff Company stand at the 1903 Leipzig Spring Toy Fair.

On the last day, so the story goes, when Richard was disconsolately packing his neglected creation away, Hermann Berg, an American buyer for the New York firm of George Borgfeldt and Co, saw Friend Petz. He was so taken with it that he ordered 3000 on the spot.

The original Friend Petz is the only early bear mis-

sing from the Steiff archives. All that remains is a blurred silhouette in a photograph of the Steiff stand at Leipzig. But the great mystery of the teddy bear world is what happened to those 3000 bears shipped to America. One possible explanation is that with their primitive string-jointed limbs they soon fell apart and were discarded by their disillusioned owners. If any did survive their historical significance means that they would be the most desirable and collectable of all teddy bears.

The teddy bear had such an immediate impact that toymakers could not keep up with the demand for them, and many new firms sprang up in England, America, and Germany. While German bears have traveled widely around the world, their American cousins were mainly produced for the increasingly extensive home market.

English manufacturers soon saw the possibility of copying the toy, as the mohair used in making it was woven in Yorkshire, and production costs could be kept down. Very little is known about most of the early English bear firms, many of which were short-lived. Factories such as William J Terry, W H Jones, and Omega Toys are known to have made bears, but their products are rarely found.

The large number of unknown manufacturers in England and America, as well as France and Eastern Europe, makes it impossible to identify every bear. Nevertheless, the following pages should cover all the major manufacturers, as well as some of the more significant types of unmarked bears.

Left: Margarete Steiff's company has some claim to have produced the first teddy bear. Steiff certainly produced bears of the highest quality.

Right: Rudolf (left) is a Steiff bear from the early 1900s. He still has his original boot-button eyes. He has had a hard life and was once shot in the voice box with an airgun! Rudolf is stuffed with Excelsior, or wood wool. Henrietta (right) is from the same era but has survived in better condition. She shows the typical Steiff profile, with boot-button eyes, very long arms, a small hump on the back, narrow ankles, and large flat feet. Henrietta shows the central head seam which one in seven Steiff bears had, a result of fabric economy (both height: 20 inches [51 cm]).

Top: An early (1905-1930s) Steiff ear button (diameter: ¼ inch [6mm]).

Above: Steiff button from the 1950s and 1960s (diameter: 3/16 inch [4 mm]).

Pre-World War I Bears: 1903-1914

Although both America and Germany have claims to be the home of the first teddy bear, documentation of German bears, particularly in the vast Steiff archives, has always made their identification easier. The Steiff Company themselves who have always enjoyed the reputation for producing the highest quality bears.

Steiff bears were distinctively identified by their famous 'Knopf im Ohr' (Button in Ear) trademark. Unfortunately for collectors, anxious parents sometimes removed the small metal ear disc. After 1908 the button was fixed over a cloth tag which gave the details of the model design and size of each bear. The color and shape of this tag changed periodically (see pages 8 and 40). The Steiff bears of this period were made in several colors, including brown, blond, gold, cinammon, white, occasionally black and, exceptionally, red. In spite of their high quality, Steiff were not above compromising for economic reasons:

one bear out of every seven had a join down the middle of the head, in order to save on fabric.

Certain features are common to most early bears, regardless of their country of manufacture. On small bears eyes were originally usually black shoe- or boot-buttons, while larger bears had specially made buttons. Around the time of World War I blown-glass eyes were introduced in Germany, and later elsewhere.

Stuffing in earlier bears was usually Excelsior, also called wood wool. This consists of lengths of shredded wood shavings originally used to pack china and glass; it is often referred to mistakenly as 'straw'. Although new materials were introduced for stuffing, Excelsior retains a firm shape over time, and was used as the material for stuffing heads up to the 1950s. After 1908 most bears were fitted with growlers which worked by tilting the animal backward and forward.

Left: Albert is an extremely fragile Steiff bear who was found, merely a bag of bits, in a cellar. His feet had rotted away, although his rusty button is still in place. He has had major restoration and wears antique clothes which both improve his appearnce and protect him from rough treatment (height: 19 inches [48 cm]).

Right: The short-pile mohair of the gold bear (left; height: 12½ inches [32 cm]) has survived in very good condition, probably because he has never benn played with. He also retains the famous Steiff 'Button in Ear' trademark. The larger blond-mohair bear (right; height: 16 inches [41 cm]) is a slightly earlier Steiff whose baldness clearly reveals his center head seam. His felt pads have been restored but he retains his original ear button. Both bears are stuffed with Excelsior. The tiny Steiff bear (height: 3½ inches [10 cm]) is fully jointed with all the features of his larger friends.

Despite these common features, there are some characteristics particular to bears according to their country of manufacture which can assist in identification. Early American and German bears have a distinctive hump on the back. This results from study of real bears whose massively developed shoulder muscles give their backs a hump-like appearance. German bears, specifically Steiff, have quite a long nose, with boot-button eyes, very long arms, a small hump, narrow ankles, and very large feet with felt pads.

English bears, on the other hand, typically have shorter arms to save fabric, boot-button eyes of lesser quality, little or no hump, and shapeless ankles (it was time-consuming to stuff narrow ankles without splitting the seams). Pads were usually thick cotton, not

Above left: Mrs Robinson, a 1904 Ideal bear, is made of beige mohair with felt footpads lined with card. Her nose and claw embroidery were originally brown thread. Her wooden boot-button eyes are rather indented as the original owner used them to teethe on!

Above: Blissful (right) is a Bruin Manufacturing Company bear wth their label stitched to his foot. He resembles other early American bears, with his triangular-shaped muzzle, boot-button eyes, and wood-wool stuffing. He is taking tea with a very rare 1920s Schuco fox (see page 35).

Left: These three bears have the Steiff profile but lack the positive identification of the Steiff ear button. The bear in clown's ruff (left; height: 21 inches [53 cm]) has a lovely long nose, small, close-set eyes, and narrow ankles. His arms are long and curved, and he has an enormous voice-box in his tummy which sadly no longer works. The small gray bear (right; height: 8 inches [20 cm]) only has feet pads. He has a well-defined nose and tiny glass eyes, a feature introduced around 1914. The seated blond bear (height: 9 inches [23 cm]) from the same era has black shoe-button eyes, and the distinctively humped back found in earlier German and American bears.

Left: Two bears from an unknown manufacturer. The smaller bear (left; height: 16 inches [41 cm]) is made from a very crude pattern. Big Theo (right; height: 28 inches [71 cm]) is a much better-made bear with typically English strong cotton pads (German bears of this period usually had felt pads).

Bottom: Miss Nightingale is an English bear of unknown manufacturer dating from around 1912. She wears a cape made for her by her original owner (height: 20 inches [51 cm]).

Below: Still Hope is identifiable as an early Aetna Toy Animal Company bear from the company name stamped on his right foot.

felt. Many firms used outworkers to keep up with their orders, and some products were quite crude, with stiff, straight arms, and completely square shoulders (see right).

Because of the clamor for teddy bears in America, many firms were established to keep up with demand. American bears of the period have large, wide-apart ears, triangular faces, a humped back, long, curved limbs, and elongated bodies. Initially all bears were made from mohair which had to be imported from Europe. As sales grew, however, production plants were soon set up in the United States.

It is rare to find an American bear of this period with a positive identification mark. Exceptions are the Bruin Manufacturing Company and the Aetna Toy Animal Company. Bruin bears sometimes have a woven label with the company's name stitched across the foot, while Aetna's early bears have an oval stamp with the company's name on the base of one card-lined felt pad.

Bears Between the Wars: 1919-1945

The outbreak of World War I had markedly different effects on the British and German toy industries, as war brought trade bans throughout Europe on German goods. Even after the war firms such as Steiff and Gebrüder Hermann, founded in 1907, found that most of their toys were being sold on the home market. The 1920s, on the other hand, were a boom period for the British industry, and many of the major bear manufacturers came into being in that decade. The British ability to fill the gap in the market left by the Germans was aided by the fact that the standard teddy-bear fabric, mohair plush, was manufactured at mills in Yorkshire, thus minimizing material and transport costs.

Well-established firms such as Dean's and J K Farnell were joined by some of the best-known names in the bear world, including Chad Valley, Chilterns, and Merrythought who were all established in the 1920s. Many other firms sprang up to meet the huge demand for bears, only to close down again with the coming of World War II in 1939.

Illustrators such as Margaret Tempest, Molly Brett, and Ernest Shepard increased the popularity of all things bear-related, and it was soon unthinkable for a child not to have a teddy as playmate and confidant. But bears were also being adopted by the adult world, aided by the arrival of literary characters such as Pooh and Rupert, whose adventures were followed by grown-ups as well as children. *Brideshead Revisited* by Evelyn Waugh demonstrates that the bear had become acceptable as a student mascot during the 1920s. The association with the famous and glamorous, such as aviator Amy Johnson, made teddy even more fashionable. Bears even became fashion accessories, such as powder compacts and scent bottles.

Although national differences in design and materials are still evident, these became less marked in later years. Bear manufacture throughout the world is

Left: Lucy (left) was originally bright pink and her companion bright gold. Both are Dean's Rag Book Company Ltd bears from the 1920s or 1930s (both height: 18 inches [46 cm]).

Inset left: Sir Edward Grey is an English bear made around 1925 (height: 23 inches [58 cm]). He was originally gray in color, of very long mohair, and has a pronounced nose which is well shaved back. His velvet suit was made for him by his original owner, who also named him, probably for Sir Edward Grey (1862-1933), sometime Liberal Foreign Secretary.

Right: A Steiff 1920s' ride-on bear (height: 16 inches [41 cm] to shoulder). The handle is a steering mechanism for the front wheels, and the ring on his side is a pull-chord for his growler. The button shows remnants of the original white tag enabling accurate dating.

Right: Bertie, a labeled Dean's bear from the 1930s (height: 26 inches [66 cm]).

Inset top: Dean's Rag Book Company label with brown lettering from the 1930s.

Inset above: Another 1930s' Dean's Rag Book Comany Ltd label.

Above far left: Two bears probably made by Steiff's great German rival, Gebrüder Hermann, founded in 1907. The bear on the left has cinammon-tipped fur (height: 15 inches [38 cm]) and his blond friend has a giant airbag in his stomach which acts as a bellows to produce a really strong 'grunt' (height: 19 inches [48 cm]).

Above center left: These two 1920s' bears are typical unmarked British bears of the period with bristly fabric, fat bodies, shapeless ankles, and shortish arms (Large bear; height: 24 inches [61 cm]; Dressed bear; height: 19 inches [48 cm]).

Above left: Happy is a 1920s Steiff bear with large glass eyes and a tipped mohair coat. She made the record books in 1989 when her owners paid £55,000 for her.

Right: Brother Ted is a jester bear bought in 1927. He is firmly stuffed with wood wool so he can stand. Of unknown maker, his glass eyes with enamel-painted backs, a cheaper alternative to blown-glass German eyes, suggest he is English (height: 19 inches [48 cm]).

marked by changes in materials; cheaper alternatives to good-quality mohair became available, and bright colors, now often faded, including pink, blue – even harlequin – were popular. Stuffing was increasingly of cheap kapok. Glass eyes with enamel coloring on the back became available as a cheaper alternative to German blown-glass eyes. This period also saw the introduction of the squeeze-type voice mechanism inside the stomach.

When the shadow of war had receded Steiff remained the dominant German manufacturer; many Steiff bears were made with tipped (two-tone) fur, a fabric popular with German manufacturers. Other German companies such as the Gebrüder Hermann also flourished. Hermann bears are difficult to identify unequivocally as the round swing-tags attached to their chests are nearly always removed. The muzzles and ear-linings of Hermann bears are nearly always made of a different fabric from the main body of the bear.

The style of British teddies from before the war is recognizable in the production of the 1920s, especially

in unmarked bears. Although some were made of good quality mohair, many were manufactured from very short pile, bristly bright gold fabric. These bears have short arms, quite fat bodies, and shapeless ankles. The ears were sometimes stuck with strong glue straight into holes in the head. The pads were made of white, off-white or flesh-pink felt, which must have been very bright when new, though beige sateen was also used.

One of the most successful and long-lived of British manufacturers has been the Dean's Rag Book Company Ltd founded in 1903. Although known mainly for their children's rag books and printed soft toys, they became established in the manufacture of mohair teddy bears around 1915-17. Dean's labels in the 1930s had brown lettering on the woven label reading 'Made in England by Dean's Rag Book Co Ltd London.' Other labels used by Dean's include white lettering on a green background in the mid 1930s, a mainly yellow label showing two dogs tearing at a rag book used in the late 1950s, and the Dean's Childsplay Toy label with a red heart from the 1960s.

OBSERVER
28 JULY 1985

A BIRTHDAY TRIBUTE
TO THE QUEEN MOTHER
85 NEXT SUNDAY

Left: Teddy Blue (left; height: 18 inches [46 cm]) is a Farnell bear from 1929. He was bright turquoise when new, and has the pale brown nose and pad embroidery used instead of black on many white and colored bears. Compton (center; height: 24 inches [61 cm]) and the small bear (height: 14 inches [36 cm]) have the unusual Farnell claws, embroidered on the pads not the backs of the paws.

Although teddy bears remained a major part of the Dean's range, their production of printed cloth toys was always important. In 1930 Walt Disney granted them the sole manufacturing rights for the first Mickey Mouse toy. Their recent production, however, has reverted to excellent replica bears, many of them taken from the company's early original patterns.

J K Farnell is a firm about which there is much speculation, as very few of its bears are ever found with labels. In existence since 1840, the company built a factory called the Alpha works shortly after World War I; this gave its name to one of their most popular lines, the Alpha bears. The construction of their bears, with center-front hand-sewn seams and strong noses, makes them the most similar to Steiff of all the British manufacturers. Indeed there have been claims that Farnell were really the inventors of the first teddy bear. Although this is unlikely, their bears are certainly of the highest quality, and they are the most distinguished of British bears.

Farnell bears were made in colors other than gold, including blue. Another distinctive feature of some Farnell bears are claws embroidered on the pad rather than the back of the paw. Farnell bears share the distinction with Steiff of being the only bears where the

Top: A labeled J K Farnell 1930s' bear. Farnell produced the highest-quality British bears, but they are rarely labeled (height: 20 inches [51 cm]). Like all Farnell bears he has feature of the last opening for stuffing being in the stomach, not the back.

Above: An 'Alpha' label from the 1930s' J K Farnell bear.

Inset left: This *Observer* magazine cover from 1985 commemorates the 85th birthday of Queen Elizabeth, the Queen Mother. The late 1930s' picture shows her carrying a teddy bear, probably a Farnell, with which she had just been presented.

Left: Rowan (left; height: 21 inches [53 cm]) is a rather worn Chad Valley bear from the 1930s. He has blown-glass eyes, wood wool throughout his head, and kapok stuffing in his body. He is very similar to the Chad Valley Magna series of bears produced at this time, and is labeled (below) on his foot. Alex (right; height; 15½ inches [39 cm]) is of the same period, but he has a button label (below) and his thick mohair coat is in much better condition. He has some wood wool in his nose, but is mainly stuffed with kapok. His large feet are lined with card, and both paw and feet pads are made of brown brushed cotton.

Below: Chad Valley label (from Rowan, above) from the 1930s.

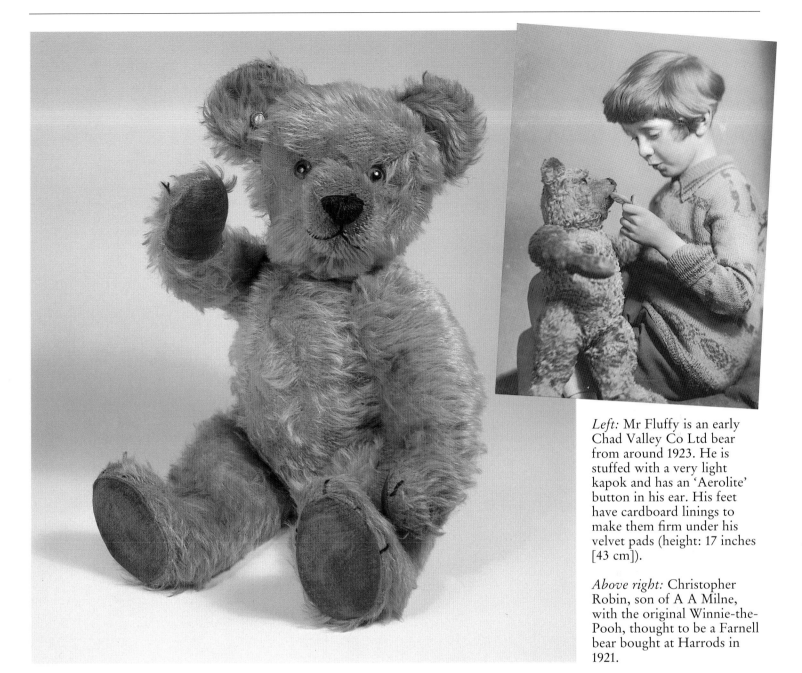

Left: Mr Fluffy is an early Chad Valley Co Ltd bear from around 1923. He is stuffed with a very light kapok and has an 'Aerolite' button in his ear. His feet have cardboard linings to make them firm under his velvet pads (height: 17 inches [43 cm]).

Above right: Christopher Robin, son of A A Milne, with the original Winnie-the-Pooh, thought to be a Farnell bear bought at Harrods in 1921.

last opening for the stuffing is in the stomach rather than the back.

It is thought that the original Winnie-the-Pooh, owned by Christopher Robin Milne, was a Farnell bear bought at Harrods in 1921. Winnie-the-Pooh is arguably the most popular bear character of all time. He first appeared in the poetry anthology *When We Were Very Young*, written by Christopher Robin's father A A Milne, and published in 1924. Although the bear was originally called Edward his name was changed to Winnie after a Black Bear in London Zoo.

Pooh's companions in the stories, Piglet, Tigger, Kanga, Roo, and Eeyore also became extremely famous in the wake of the books' success. The original toy characters from the stories, apart from Roo, who was lost, are now on display in the New York Public Library.

While Pooh may have been a Farnell, the bear in Ernest Shepard's famous illustrations is based on Growler, a Steiff bear belonging to Shepard's son. The popularity of the characters was renewed when Disney produced its first Winnie-the-Pooh cartoon in 1966, and in 1975 a full-length feature film was made, which still fills cinemas today.

The Chad Valley Company Ltd of Wellington, Shropshire, was formed in 1920; it was one of Britain's leading toy manufacturers until quite recently. An early identification mark was the 'Aerolite' button in the ear, which reads 'Chad Valley "Aerolite" Trademark.' Later bears were marked by a label on the foot reading 'Hygienic Toys made in England by the Chad Valley Company Ltd' or by a button in the ear covered with celluloid, and reading, 'Chad Valley Hygienic Toys.' The use of buttons as trademarks was clearly never completely confined to Steiff. Other firms tried at various times to use this clever labelling device, but were eventually forced to revert to foot labels by lawyers acting for the Steiff company.

Left: Chummy (left; height: 21 inches [53 cm]) is a Merrythought bear from the 1930s. He is stuffed with kapok with some straw in his nose. His pads are made of dull orange felt with the maker's label (top) sewn in the right foot, and celluloid-covered button (above) in his left ear. The paw embroidery is interesting and shows the connection, through Merrythought's founder A C Janisch, with Farnell. Colin (right; height: 21 inches [53 cm]) is an early Merrythought bear from the Magnet range. He has the same identification marks as Chummy, but his button is in his left shoulder.

Left: This lovely 1930s' Peacock Bear (height: 20 inches [51 cm]) is one of the few that survive from this English firms. His label (inset right) is attached to his right foot and is embroidered in red silk.

Above right: These Bingie Boy (right; height: 19 inches [48 cm]) and Girl (left; height: 15 inches [38 cm]) bears have velveteen doll-type bodies, with mohair on the head and lower arms. They both have labels of the bases of their cardboard-lined feet. Ears are lined with 'art silk plush.'

Right: The Chad Valley Cubby bear (right; height: 13 inches [33 cm]) was made in two contrasting fabrics and is similar to the Merrythought Bingie bear cub (left; height: 12 inches).

Many English bears from the 1930s to the late 1950s had Rexine pads. This was the tradename of a type of oilcloth which simulated leather, and gives many people the impression that teddy bears should have leather pads.

Several firms around this time produced 'cub' type bears, with unjointed hips but movable arms, among them the Merrythought Company. This firm was founded in 1930 when C J Rendel of Chad Valley and A C Janisch of Farnell joined the existing mohair production company of Holmes and Laxton, based at Ironbridge in Shropshire. Many of the Chad Valley workers followed Rendel to the new company, which used as its trademark a wishbone combined with the word 'Merrythought'. One of their greatest assets was the deaf-mute Florence Atwood. She was the company's chief designer until her death in 1949.

Left: These three bears, although unlabeled. were almost certainly made by the Chiltern Hygienic Toy Company. Trevor (center; height: 24 inches [61 cm]) is a very large bear, and was obviously never played with, since he has survived in perfect condition. His well-shaved nose is stuffed with wood wool, the rest of his body with kapok. He has beige velvet pads, with cardboard inner soles to help him stand. The little white bear (right; height: 15 inches [38 cm]) has clear glass eyes which would originally have had brown enamel painted on the back. The skating bear (left; height 15 inches [38 cm]) was made in several sizes, and also in blue. When they have lost their muffs they are quite often mistaken for page boys.

Some early Merrythought bears reveal the connection with Farnell through their founder A C Janisch in the interesting paw embroidery. Early Merrythought bears have both a makers' label 'Merrythought Hygienic Toys – Made in England,' sewn into the right foot and a celluloid-covered button is in the left ear reading 'Hygienic Merrythought Toys, Made in England,' with the wishbone emblem also stamped on. Others had a button positioned on the back of the left shoulder in an attempt to circumvent Steiff's 'Button in Ear' trademark.

The 'Bingie' range of bears produced in the 1930s by Merrythought was a series of novelty bears, many of them dressed in elaborate costumes. All Bingie bears had ear-linings of synthetic 'art silk plush' – a new fabric also used for a complete range of bears.

The history of Peacock's, another English firm of the period, is relatively obscure. They were based in London, and taken over by Chad Valley in 1931. Their bears are similar in many ways to the standard Chad Valley series of the early 1930s.

One of the most popular bears of the 1930s, were those produced by a major manufacturer for mail-order catalogues and department stores. These teddies are never found with an identification mark, and were made in all sizes from around 8 inches to 25 inches (20cm to 63cm). Because these bears were manufactured en masse for a variety of outlets, they never had sewn-on labels, but were individually marked with either chest tags or adhesive labels. As these are easily separated from the bear, firm identification becomes almost impossible.

The Chiltern company was formed by H G Stone and Leon Rees, and the brand-name Chiltern was registered in 1924. Chiltern continued in production for many years. Both before and after World War II it is likely that they manufactured many of the unlabelled department store-type bears of the period. In 1967 they were taken over by Chad Valley, and around this time bears were produced with both company names combined on the label.

American firms continued successfully to make traditional bears throughout the teddy-bear boom of the interwar years. One such maker was the Knickerbocker Toy Co, founded in the early 1900s. Their early bears are marked with a woven label sewn into the center-front seam or the left ear. Later products were labeled on the left-side seam.

Although traditional 1930s bears were still available in some British shops for the early part of World War II, toy manufacturers were soon required to produce more essential items, as supplies of fabrics also dropped off. Typically, therefore, wartime teddies were home-made, many being made from old blankets or other recyclable fabric, as fur fabrics became scarce. Magazines and newspapers produced patterns which showed a simple outline of a bear for construction at home (see pages 2-3).

Left: This fascinating gas-mask holder was obviously made professionally by someone whose factory had turned to making barrage balloons, as the holder appears to be made of that fabric (height: 10 inches [26 cm]).

Above: Senior Mr Roosevelt is a Knickerbocker Toy Company bear. He has a muzzle made from short-pile mohair and beige velvet pads. He is in extremely good condition and stuffed with kapok throughout.

Left: These two bears are unlabeled and are typical British mail-order bears from the 1930s. The bear on the left (height: 20 inches [51 cm]) was pale blue when new. The larger bear, Bunty (height: 25 inches [63 cm]), is completely stuffed with wood wool, although most only have this in the head and kapok in the body. The pads, which have nearly always worn through, were made of a brushed cotton flanelette-type material in flesh pink.

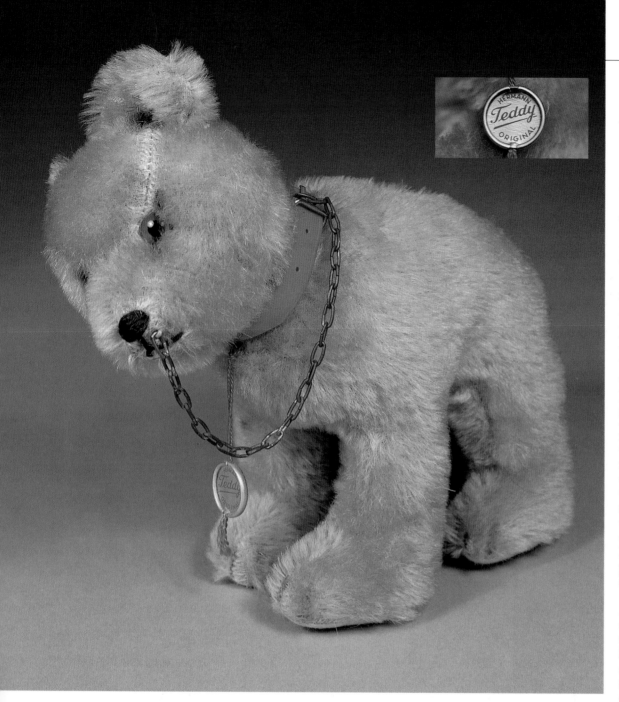

Left: This 1950s' Gebruder Hermann standing bear has a plastic collar and swivel head. He retains his original chest tag (inset; diameter: 5/8 inch [15 mm]) of a type introduced in 1952, with red lettering on one side and gold on the other. Unlike many of his contemporaries he is made of gold mohair plush so has survived in excellent condition.

Below far left: Three postwar bears of unknown origin. The bear in the boater (left; height: 13 inches [33 cm]) and the small bear (right; height: 9 inches [23 cm]) are of cotton-rayon with wood-wool stuffing, and may be of East European origin. The larger beige bear (height: 13½ inches [34 cm]) is made of a very simialr cotton-rayon fabric. It was bought in Germany in 1950, and the voice box has strong similarities to Steiff voices of the period. The overall quality of the bear, with its long arms and traditional profile, puts it in a different class from the others.

Below left: These two unmarked German bears of the 1950s would originally have had paper chest tags sewn on. The larger bear (left; height: 23 inches [58 cm]) is made of a very violent shade of gold mohair. He has hard linings to his feet and can stand by himself. He has contrasting muzzle and pads. The two-tone bear (right; height: 21 inches [53 cm]) is made of a tipped cinammon synthetic plush, again with ear linings and nose from a different, shorter-pile fabric.

Right: A 1930s' Norah Wellings pink velvet nightdress case with bear head and hands (right; height: 17 inches [43 cm]) labeled (inset above) on the foot. The Wendy Boston bear (left; height 14½ inches [37 cm]) is one of her early unjointed designs from around 1950. It is made of mohair stuffed with kapok and sports (inset below) an unusual red, white, and blue label.

Bears Since the War: 1945-1970

After the difficulties of the war years, by around 1948 the toy industry was resuming production. Many new synthetic fabrics which had been experimented with before the war came into full use as did plastic eyes and noses. The two gold bears (left) are typical of many bears of the postwar period. Cotton-rayon has replaced more expensive mohair, joints are fixed crudely with wire, and the wood-wool stuffing gives the impression that the bears are earlier than they are.

High-quality bears continued to be made, using traditional materials and robust constructional techniques, usually by long-established firms such as Steiff and Gebrüder Hermann. An important development, later encouraged by toy safety regulations, was the introduction of lock-in safety eyes, first patented by Wendy Boston for her synthetic washable bears in 1948.

Wendy Boston and Norah Wellings were two of

Left: Merrythought's 1957 range of bears included Mr Twisty-Cheeky (left; height: 10 inches [26 cm]) made with a wire frame in his body so that it can be twisted and turned. The clothes are made of nylon suede, and his head of mohair plush. The small gold Cheeky (right; height: 9 inches [23 cm]) is of similar construction. The largest Cheeky (height: 15 inches [38 cm]) is made of synthetic plush, with a velvet nose. He has bells in his large ears to amuse a child.

Above: 1957 Merrythought label.

Above center: 1960s' Merrythought label.

Above right: This cinammon bear was probably manufactured by the Gaeltarra Eireann company who also traded under the name Tara Toys. He has wood wool throughout his head and body and (top right) a small red-and-white foot label reading 'Made in the Republic of Ireland; before 1949 it would have read 'Made in Eire.'

the most prominent bear designers and manufacturers. Norah Wellings had worked at Chad Valley before leaving to start her own business. She is best known for her velvet doll designs which she made at her factory in Wellington, Shropshire, from 1926 to 1960. Most Norah Wellings toys are identified by a woven silk label with black lettering.

Wendy Boston was one of the most prolific and successful of teddy-bear makers after World War II. Her early designs were unjointed and made of mohair stuffed with kapok, versions after c. 1954-55 being of synthetic fabric stuffed with foam. The long-established firm of Merrythought were also capable of innovation. Their range of 'Cheeky' Bears have broad heads, unusual velvet noses, and safety eyes.

Bear production began in Ireland after World War II with the establishment of the Gaeltarra Eireann company who also traded under the name Tara Toys. This was a state-sponsored industry started in the late 1940s, and many of their bears were exported to Britain and the United States.

The status of the teddy bear can be judged by the award in 1938 of a Royal Warrant to Chad Valley by the present Queen Mother. Bears made before 1952 can be dated by the wording 'By Appointment to Her

Majesty Queen Elizabeth.' By taking over the Chiltern company in 1967, Chad Valley became the largest soft-toy manufacturer in Britain. Their fortunes, however, declined rapidly during the 1970s. They were eventually bought by Palitoy in 1978, and in 1980 the last of their factories was closed. The Chad Valley name was dormant until 1988 when it was bought by Woolworths who now use it on a range of imported soft toys from the Far East. Traditional Chad Valley bears are no longer made.

Other well-known firms producing bears in the 1950s were Pedigree Soft Toys and Lefray Toys. Pedigree was a subsidiary of Lines Brothers Ltd. The firm started manufacturing bears before the war at the Triang works in Merton, but many were made at their Belfast factory, opened in 1946. In the 1950s Lefray produced traditional-style jointed bears with velvet pads; still in business they now make unjointed modern-style bears.

Sooty, one of the most endearing of bear characters, was first seen on British television in 1952. Chad Valley were licenced to produce a glove puppet, while Chiltern Toys produced Sooty on a tricycle. Rupert the Bear is another much-loved British cartoon character. The adventures of Rupert first appeared in the *Daily Express* in 1920, and the stories have been translated into many languages; he is particularly popular in the Netherlands.

Top: This group portrait presents a good selection of bears of various ages and sizes.

Above: Chad Valley label from between 1938, when the company received the Royal Warrant, and 1952 when the Queen became the Queen Mother.

Right: This 1950s' gold Pedigree bear (left; height: 13 inches [33 cm]) has a coat of wool-mohair mixture, brown-velvet pads, and glass eyes. The label (inset right) is fixed into the side seam. The traditional gold and cinammon jointed Lefray bear (right) has velvet pads and also dates from the 1950s.

The stories of Rupert were first drawn by Mary Tourtel, who continued illustrating the cartoon strip and associated books until her retirement in 1935. The appearance of Rupert has changed from his early colors of blue jumper and gray check trousers and scarf to the more familiar red and yellow he wears today.

Alfred Bestall continued to draw the strip for the next thirty years, and was also responsible for the highly successful Rupert Annuals launched in 1936. One of the most celebrated Bestall illustrations inspired the Paul McCartney and Geoffrey Dunbar 1984 video 'Rupert and the Frog Song.' Since 1965 Rupert has continued to be popular, though now drawn by a team of artists. A 'Friends of Nutwood' fan club exists, and there have been two separate television series.

Smokey the Bear is probably the best known bear in America. He was created in 1944 as the emblem of the Forest Fire Prevention campaign, and was first used only on posters. Early pictures show him unclothed, but he was soon given his familiar denim jeans and ranger hat. The character rapidly became so popular that licenses for Smokey products were issued in 1952.

The Ideal Toy Company, founded by Teddy Bear pioneer Morris Michtom, produced the first Smokey Bear toy in 1953. Later Smokeys have also been made by other firms, such as Dakin and the Knickerbocker Toy Company, and the bear continues to play a great part in preventing forest fires throughout the United States.

Many National Parks and tourist areas, such as Yellowstone, also sold miniature bear toys and ornaments as mementoes. The bear as an emblem of America and Canada evokes mixed feelings. In many areas they have become troublesome – Polar bears and other Brown and Kodiak bears frequently raid dustbins. The common Black bear is so familiar to people in some regions that they often forget these are dangerous wild animals, responsible for 80% of the continent's bear attacks.

Rangers in the National Parks cannot stop these attacks totally, especially in cases where tourist stupidity provokes the animal. However, the introduction of special feeding areas to keep the bears away from human rubbish dumps, and the removal of persistent offenders to bear sanctuaries, coupled with the bear's natural restraint, ensure that human casualties are kept to a minimum.

Left: In the 1950s Chiltern Toys were licensed to produce Sooty on a tricycle (right; height: 10½ inches [27 cm]). When pulled by the string the tricycle wheel moves Sooty's legs, giving the impression that he is pedaling. The glove puppet (left; height: 8 inches [20 cm]) is a Chad Valley production. Rupert Bear, seen here in bendy-toy form (center; height: 10½ inches [27 cm]), first appeared in a cartoon in the *Daily Express* in 1920.

Top: 1950s' Chiltern Toys label from Sooty on a tricycle (left).

Above: Post-1952 Chad Valley label from bear on page 28.

Above right: Smokey the Bear was created in 1944 as an emblem of the Forest fire Prevention Campaign. This example is a more recent one by Dakin (height: 13 inches [33 cm]).

Right: This black bear with red collar is a souvenir brought back from the Great Smoky Mountains, an area of National Park in North Carolina (height to shoulder: 5½ inches [14 cm]).

Novelty and Mechanical Bears

Mechanical bears are as much a branch of automata as teddy-bear production, and many were made by manufacturers of mechanical toys. One such firm was the German makers Schreyer and Co, known by the abbreviation Schuco, who were established in 1912. Most were not stuffed in the usual way. Among the best products of the Schuco factory were 'Yes' and 'No' bears, whose heads are operated by moving the tail. Schuco also produced small bears formed from a metal framework covered with mohair plush, folded and fixed into place with glue or by stitching.

The very tiniest bears from the early 1930s had little felt hands and feet staples on to the ends of the limbs, and were made in a variety of very bright colors, including red, green, and blue. Later versions of these bears were made without the tiny hands and feet, and were slightly clumsier in shape. Schuco made some soft bears in a variety of sizes. They were produced with pads, ear-linings, and muzzles of short-pile mohair in a color either matching or contrasting with the body. The smaller soft-bodied Schuco bears have a very simple jointing mechanism of wire threaded through the body.

Japan became the world leaders in cheap, brightly

Left and below far left: A selection of Schuco bears (heights: 2½, 4½, 7, 5½ inches [6, 12, 18, 14 cm]).

Centre below left: The large cinammon somersaulting acrobat bear (left; height: 14 inches [35 cm]), made by the German firm of Bing around 1910, is wound by turning the left arm. He is then hung on the frame to perform. The little clockwork clown bear (height: 10 inches [26 cm]), which swings a ball and a stick to rotate the colored balls, was almost certainly imported to England by Moses Kohnstamm of Furth, Germany, in the 1920s.

Below left: Schuco 'Yes and No' bears (large height: 15 inches [38 cm]/ small height: 5 inches [13 cm])

Right: Two Japanese clockwork mechanical bears, probably from the 1950s. The knitting bear (right; height: 6 inches [15 cm]) moves her hands to simulate knitting. The other has magnets in his hands to lift and turn the metal pages of his book (height: 7 inches [18 cm]).

Far left: When the key on this small Japanese clockwork bear is wound up it lumbers forward in an ungainly fashion, stops, emits a high-pitched roar, and moves off again (height to shoulders: 4 inches [10 cm]).

Left: This nodding-head advertising bear was bought at a trade show in Germany in the 1950s. It was used to advertise Maynard's Wine Gums for many years. Its head tilts back and forward, and its mouth opens and closes. The whole mechanism is operated by a mercury switch (height: 22 inches [56 cm]).

Left: Yogi Bear (height: 16½ inches [42 cm]).

Above right: This group illustrates the diversity of soft animals that have been manufactured at various times. It includes two Steiff koalas (height: 4½ and 6 inches [11 and 15 cm]), a Pilkie nightdress-case Panda (height: 17 inches [43 cm]) and a small Polar Bear on all fours, made of synthetic plush (height to shoulder: 6½ inches [16 cm]). The large standing Polar Bear is based on a real Polar bear called Ivy at London Zoo in the 1950s who had a well-known cub called Brumus (height: 19 inches [48 cm]).

Above far right: This Paddington Bear sports duffel coat and hat as described in Michael Bond's books made by Gabrielle Designs (height: 19 inches [48 cm]). The original of Nookie Bear (height: 21 inches [53 cm]) is ventriloquist Roger de Courcey's assistant.

Right: The bear in the shawl (height: 13 inches [33 cm]) dates from around 1912 and has a pill-box rattle. The 1950s' Chiltern bear (right; height 12 inches [30 cm]) has a revolving rattle in his stomach. The Leco bear (left; height: 12 inches [30 cm]) has a key-wound musical movement which also turns his head from side to side.

colored clockwork toys after World War II. The majority of faces on bear toys are somewhat unrealistic, but they have become highly collectable nevertheless.

Paddington became famous in 1958 when Michael Bond's first book, *A Bear Called Paddington*, was published. As with other famous character bears, the books have been translated into many languages, and Paddington has appeared in his own television series shown in several countries. The first Paddington toy

was produced by Gabrielle designs in 1972. The American version of Paddington was manufactured by Eden Toys Inc.

Another popular character is Nookie Bear who rose to fame in Britain when he appeared with ventriloquist Roger de Courcey on a television talent show. He still appears in cabaret, television ads, and, very occasionally, in theater performances.

Yogi Bear is the most outstanding of the many bears who have featured in American animated television series. He was created by the famous Hanna-Barbera animation studios, and named after a popular baseball player. With his friends Booboo and Cindy he roamed the mountains of Jellystone National Park, seeking out hapless picnickers, and making off with their food.

Many bears have musical movements or rattles in their stomachs. Some early bears have a rattle formed from a pill box containing cut-out metal circles. A later device was a revolving rattle in the stomach, which would keep a child amused for a long time.

Leco were a short-lived company which made toys in London between 1955 and 1971. Like many British firms at this time, their bears were produced in sheepskin, resulting in a very soft, but somewhat shapeless toy. Over the years, the skin becomes dry and brittle, and most bears deteriorate badly.

A collection usually includes some koalas, pandas, and polar bears. Often in England these were associated with real animals living in London Zoo at the time. Brumus the famous bear cub of the 1950s, and his mother Ivy, were responsible for a flood of polar bear toys at that time.

Bear Collecting Today: 1970s-Present

The ancestor of the teddy bear, the brown bear Ursus Arctos, has awed and fascinated men ever since prehistoric times. Many myths surround wild bears, one of them being that the babies were born as amorphous lumps, which the mother licked into the shape of cubs. This gave rise to the expression of children being 'licked into shape' by their parents. The bear's obvious intelligence, apparently human emotions, and ability to walk on two legs have led to our high respect for it. Indeed, when Darwin's *Origin of the Species* suggested mankind's evolution from apes, a rival theory was put forward that we had in fact evolved from bears instead.

In all his ninety years, the teddy bear has never been more popular than he is now. He is a perennial favorite in children's nursery rhymes and books, and has ever-increasing legions of adult admirers. The 1980s saw a massive boom in the bear industry, not just in manufacturing, but also in a whole host of associated activities. The first specialist bear museums in

Left: Happy is a Steiff bear whose owners paid a record £55,000 for her in 1989. She travels around the world with them as a teddy bear ambassador.

Right: This Dresden figurine (height: 6½ inches [17 cm]) depicts the actor Peter Bull whose 1969 book *The Teddy Bear Book* gave great impetus to the serious study and collecting of teddy bears.

Below: This label identifies the bears produced by the House of Nisbet, a doll-making business which since 1978 has produced some of the most interesting collectors' bears, including a replica of Peter Bull's own bear, Aloysius (overleaf).

Britain and America opened early in the decade, and there are now many more all over the world, as well as hundreds of specialist bear shops.

The increased prices for bears at auction have made newspaper headlines across the globe. The world record of £220 ($450) in 1978 paid for Shirley Temple's bear from the 1936 movie *Captain January*, seems insignificant compared to the current world record £55,000 ($86,350) paid by Paul and Rosemary Volpp for their two-tone Steiff bear 'Happy' at Sotheby's, London in 1989. With such a leap in value over little more than a decade, bears are being seen as a sound financial investment.

Although bears have never fallen in popularity as a childrens' toy, Arctophilia, and the collecting of teddy bears as a serious hobby for adults was ignited by the publication in 1969 of *The Teddy Bear Book* written by the British actor the late Peter Bull. This led to a wave of public nostalgia, and many people who had forgotten their bears since childhood took them out of the attic, brushed them down, and found that the charm of their old friend increased their desire to obtain others. High profile collectors such as the Volpps and Peter Bull have frequently appeared in the media, and brought many new arctophiles into the bear world.

While antique teddies have become increasingly difficult to find at reasonable prices, the replica bears

from major manufacturers and the boom in handmade artist bears have opened up new fields for collectors. Peter Bull's affection for teddy bears influenced many people, among them Alison Wilson, designer for the House of Nisbet. This firm started in 1953 as a doll-making business, but in 1978 widened its scope, and began to make teddy bears. They produced some interesting collectors' bears, including Bully Bear, a set of Zodiac Bears, and a replica of Peter Bull's own bear, Aloysius. Their bears are identified by a distinctive label on the left foot.

Bears have featured in the folklore of many countries for centuries. The story of Goldilocks and the Three Bears, published for the first time in the early 1830s, is the most famous of all bear stories, and has inspired many toys and books. Card games, parlor games, jigsaw puzzles, and building blocks all feature beautiful illustrations of the family of bears. After the birth of the teddy bear, many manufacturers brought out novelty items involving both teddies and real bears.

There are many bear-related items which can be collected, sometimes more easily than actual teddies. Carved wooden bears from the Black Forest area of Germany are particularly charming, and come in all sizes from ¼ inch (6mm) high to giant 7ft (2.1m)-high hallstands. They were usually brought home by tourists visiting the area, where hand-carving has always been a traditional craft. Carved wooden bears

Left: The story of the *Three Bears* was first published in the 1830s and has inspired much memorabilia including this book (8½x11 inches [22x28 cm]) and jigsaw (17x11 inches [45x28 cm]).

Below left: Aloysius/ Delicatessen is a bear that has many connexions with both England and America. He was made around 1907, probably by the Ideal Toy Company, and had lived all his life in a dried-goods store before being given to the British actor and arctophile Peter Bull who christened him Delicatessen. His moment of glory came in 1981 when he played the part of Sebastian Flyte's teddy bear Aloysius in the Granada Television dramatization of Evelyn Waugh's novel *Brideshead Revisited.* After Peter Bull's death he returned to America.

Above right: Bear novelties come in a seemingly infinite variety of guises including this lighter (left; height: 3 inches [7 cm]), teething ring (center; height: 2 inches [5 cm]), match case (height: 3 inches [7 cm]), glass bottle (height: 6 inches [15 cm]), and chocolate card (4½ a 3 inches [11.5x8 cm]).

Right: Bear-related wooden items from the Black Forest in Germany come in many different forms including this ashtray (height: 6 inches [15 cm]) and nutcrackers (height: 7½ inches [19 cm]).

Left: This array of modern American bears includes a Knickerbocker Toy Company bear wearing a hat (height: 15 inches [38 cm]), a Toyland Ltd Polar Bear (height: 17 inches [43 cm]), and a North American Bear Company oatmeal bear (height: 7 inches [18 cm]). Today few major manufacturers produce a product which is appealing to collectors who still prefer the traditional teddy bear.

Below left: Gebrüder Hermann bears designed by American bear artists. Sally, the white bear (height: 10 inches [25 cm]), was designed by Jenny Krantz in a limited edition of 2000. Robin Hood, or the Sherwood Bear (height: 17 inches [45 cm]), was designed by Joyce-Ann Haughey. Both these modern Hermann bears carry the bright red plastic chest tag (inset) which is currently the firm's trademark (diameter varies: 3/4 or 1½ inches [18 or 36 mm]).

Right: Steiff are in the fortunate position of having an extensive archive from their earliest days, which they use as a basis for their excellent replica bears. One of their most successful is this cinammon bear (left; height: 20½ inches [52 cm]), Bär 35 PB, who is a copy of the earliest bear in the archive. The gray Richard Steiff bear (right; height: 12 inches [30 cm]) is a 1983 replica of the bear designed by Richard Steiff in 1905. Although not a limited edition this replica has become one of the most sought-after bears in the collectors' range. The tiny white bear (height: 6½ inches [16 cm]) is a replica of Petsy, first produced in 1927.

Below: A Steiff limited-edition button and label.

are found in other countries, such as Russia, but their quality is never as high as the German-Swiss work. The sentimental appeal of the bear has also led to its appearance in many different forms, from teething rings to scent bottles.

While the collectors market for bears became increasingly significant throughout the 1970s, the major toy manufacturers at this time found that their modern products were not as appealing as traditional teddy bears to the more discerning customer. Many famous manufacturers, such as the Knickerbocker Toy Company were producing items which had little appeal for the serious bear collector, and even the largest firms such as Steiff found their fortunes were instantly revived when they introduced replicas of their early toys.

Since the early 1980s, the Steiff firm have made re-plicas of many of their antique bears. They are extremely lucky in that their archive of toys survived both World Wars almost intact. Possibly the best replica so far is the recent cinammon 'Bär 35 PB,' a copy of the earliest surviving bear in the company archive. His joints are held together by string, as he predated the introduction of disc-type joints linked by cotter-pins on Richard Steiff's improved prototype of 1905 – the little gray bear whose design became the basis of Steiff's production in an almost unaltered state until 1951, although only the first two examples were made in gray mohair plush.

Modern Steiff bears carry a shiny brass button considerably larger than those used on antique bears. The tags on the limited edition bears are normally white (see left), while those on the standard production lines are bright yellow.

Left: Two limited edition British collectors' bears: the Merrythought 'Touch of Silk' bear (left; height: 18 inches [46 cm]) limited to 1000 examples, the Dean's Rag Book Company 'Walter' (height: 15 inches [38 cm]) was a very popular bear limited to 1500.

Below left: A French Kodiak bear (height: 26 inches [67 cm]), an example of the arctophilia that swept France in 1988 following the popularity of Jean-Jacques Annaud's film *The Bear*.

Many other firms now produce replica bears. Hermann, one of Steiff's main competitors, have commissioned American bear artists to design outstanding original bears, while also producing replicas from their own archives. Many new bears utilize new forms of stuffing which give the bear a softer feel, and make it more posable.

The teddy-bear lover's addiction is catered for by many Bear conventions, or 'Bearfests,' and festivals around the world, as well as several specialist magazines, and some spectacular books! The most well-known is probably the annual Walt Disney World Teddy Bear Convention. However, it is important to remember that people collect bears at every imaginable level. Young children and teenagers fill their bedrooms with collections of soft unjointed friends, and St Valentine's day has become associated with the sending of teddy bears as well as red roses. Bears are quite often exchanged between brides and bridegrooms, and young married couples may collect a few, as their finances permit.

In 1988 Jean-Jaques Annaud's true-life adventure film *The Bear* took France by storm, and many replica wild bears were produced, creating an alternative to the teddy for French arctophiles. While the film raised

Left: A teddy bears' tea party attended by, left to right, Oscar (height: 11 inches [28 cm]), Clarence (height: 12 inches [31 cm]), and Pooh (height: 11 inches [28 cm]).

Below: Following the success of American bear artists, some British collectors and enthusiasts have begun creating their own artist bears. These are two examples of the author's work, Bumbletoes (left; height: 26 inches [66 cm]) and a tiny gold bear (height: 6½ inches [16 cm]).

awareness of the plight of bears, and was successful at the British cinema, the jointed teddy is still second to none for English bear-lovers.

Major English manufacturers Merrythought and Dean's have both been in the forefront of the production of replica bears. Bear artists also abound in England, and the example of American creativity has encouraged British craftsmen to produce many unusual and successful bears. The scarcity of antique bears has encouraged would-be collectors to buy new artist bears in preference to mediocre examples of old bears at over-inflated prices.

However, it is once their families have grown up that the majority of collectors suddenly feel the urge to recreate their own childhood. Nostalgia plays a large part – the memories evoked by holding in one's hands some small part of the past are a unique experience. Of course many others never pack their childhood toys away in the attic, and can eventually devote whole areas or even complete houses to their collections. Whether you collect really early German bears and their accessories, or just want to give your childhood companions a treat, there is nothing better than to put them in a miniature room setting and watch them enjoying their tea party.

Collecting bears is an engrossing pastime which leads to many new friendships. After a time, some collectors start to experiment with fabrics, and a few have become renowned bear artists. Whatever direction a collector follows, there is a sense of unity among arctophiles perhaps unequalled in history.

Places To See Bears

Great Britain

The Bear Museum,
38 Dragon St, Petersfield, Hants GU31 4JJ
0730 265108

The Museum of Childhood, London
081-981 1711

Cotswold Teddy Bear Museum,
Broadway, Worcs
0386 858323

The Teddy Bear Museum,
14 Greenhill St, Stratford-upon-Avon, Warks
0789 293160

USA

The Margaret Woodbury Strong Museum,
Rochester, New York

Germany

Margarete Steiff Museum,
Giengen, Germany

Australia

Romy's Bazaar
2 Badgery's Crescent, Lawson 2783

Acknowledgments

The publisher would like to thank David Eldred who designed this book, Liz Montgomery, the picture researcher, and Aileen Reid, the editor. We would also like to thank the following individuals, agencies and institutions for supplying the illustrations:

The Bear Museum, 38 Dragon Street, Petersfield, Hampshire/Photography Nick Nicholson, Hawkeley Studios, 3 Weston Close, Bellfield Road, Godalming, Surrey: Pages 5, 7, 8 (main picture), 9, 10 (below left), 11 (above left and below right), 12 (both), 13, 14 (top left, top center, and below), 15, 16-17, 17 (above right), 18 (main picture), 19 (above left), 20 (both left), 21 (both), 22, 23 (both left), 24 (above left, both below), 25, 26-27, 27 (right), 28 (above left), 28-29, 30, 31 (both right), 32 (all 4), 33, 34 (all 3), 35 (all 3), 37, 38 (above), 39 (both), 40 (both left), 41, 42 (both), 43 (both)/Photography J Sparrow: pages 8 (top right and above right), 14 (both left), 17 (right), 18 (below right), 20 (top right, above right, and below right), 24 (top right), 25 (above right and right), 27 (top 30), 28 (all 3 below right), 31 (both above left), 36 (below right), 40 (inset left and below right)

Observer Newspapers/Photography Nick Nicholson: page 19 (below right)

Smithsonian Institution, Washington DC: page 4

Margarete Steiff GmbH: page 6

Paul and Rosemary Volpp, Buena Park, California: pages 10 (top 2), 11 (right), 14 (top right), 23 (above right), 36, 38 (below)